HEALTHY CHOICES

Lunch

Vic Parker

raintree

Raintree is an imprint of Capstone Global Library
Limited, a company incorporated in England and Wales
having its registered office at 7 Pilgrim Street, London,
EC4V 6LB – Registered company number: 6695582

www.raintreepublishers.co.uk
myorders@raintreepublishers.co.uk

Edited by Rebecca Rissman, Dan Nunn,
   and Diyan Leake
Designed by Philippa Jenkins
Original illustrations © Capstone Global
   Library Ltd 2014
Picture research by Tracy Cummins
Production by Helen McCreath
Originated by Capstone Global Library Ltd
Printed and bound in China

ISBN 978 1 406 27196 6 (hardback)
17 16 15 14 13
10 9 8 7 6 5 4 3 2 1

ISBN 978 1 406 27201 7 (paperback)
18 17 16 15 14
10 9 8 7 6 5 4 3 2 1

Parker, Vic
Lunch (Healthy Choices)
A full catalogue record for this book is available from
the British Library.

Acknowledgements
We would like to thank the following for permission to
reproduce photographs: Capstone Publishers (Karon
Dubke) pp. 4, 6, 7, 8, 9, 10, 11, 14, 15, 16, 17, 18,
19, 20, 21, 22, 23, 24, 25, 26, 27; Getty Images
p. 5 (Elie Bernager); Istockphoto p. 12 (© Paweł
Bartkowski); Shutterstock p. 13 (© MSPhotographic).

Cover photograph of a pepperoni pizza reproduced
with permission of Shutterstock (© Joe Gough) and
a grilled chicken and spinach salad reproduced with
permission of Getty Images (Joseph De Leo).

Every effort has been made to contact copyright
holders of material reproduced in this book. Any
omissions will be rectified in subsequent printings if
notice is given to the publisher.

All the internet addresses (URLs) given in this book were
valid at the time of going to press. However, due to the
dynamic nature of the internet, some addresses may
have changed, or sites may have changed or ceased to
exist since publication. While the author and publisher
regret any inconvenience this may cause readers, no
responsibility for any such changes can be accepted by
either the author or the publisher.

Contents

 Some words are shown in bold, **like this.** You can find out what they mean by looking in the glossary.

Why make healthy choices?

Just as computers run on electricity, your body runs on food and water. You need food and water in order to think, move, and grow. Healthy foods contain more goodness for your body than unhealthy foods. If you make healthy choices, you will feel and look your best.

Try to drink at least six glasses of plain water every day.

Eating unhealthily can make you feel tired and grumpy.

To work properly, your body needs different kinds of foods in the right amounts for your age and size. People who eat healthy foods have plenty of energy. They are ill less often than those who eat unhealthy foods.

What makes a lunch healthy or unhealthy?

It is important to eat lunch to keep up our energy levels in the middle of the day. Some lunch foods are much less healthy than others. For instance, chips are usually high in **saturated fat,** which can clog up your heart and blood vessels.

Chicken noodle soup from a tin is often high in **sodium**, which is bad for your heart.

a slice of thin-crust vegetarian pizza
200 calories

a slice of stuffed-crust pepperoni pizza
400 calories

The energy food gives us is measured in **calories.** You need a certain amount of calories per day to stay healthy, depending on your age, your height, and how much exercise you do. Eating too many or too few calories every day can make us **overweight** or too thin.

Savoury sandwiches

A sandwich may look healthy but it can be packed with unhealthy ingredients. White bread lacks **fibre,** which keeps your stomach working. It is low in **vitamins** and **minerals,** which your body needs to grow and to repair itself. Fillings made from **processed** foods can be high in **saturated fat** and **sodium.**

A sandwich can contain more fat and calories than some people should eat in a day.

fatty mayonnaise

white bread

processed cheese

processed meat

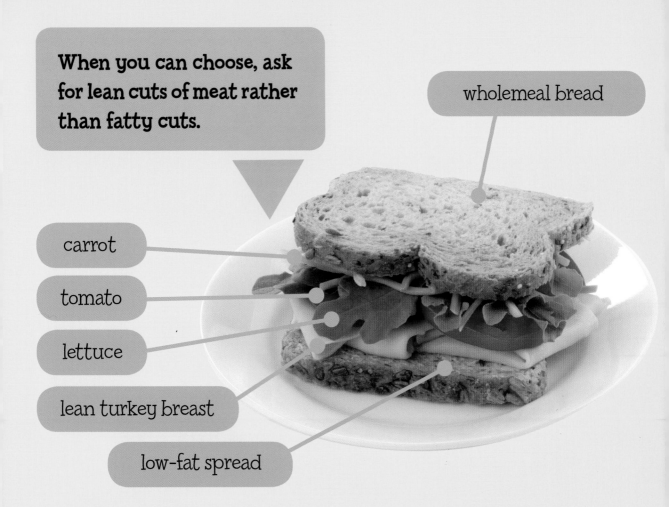

When you can choose, ask for lean cuts of meat rather than fatty cuts.

wholemeal bread

carrot

tomato

lettuce

lean turkey breast

low-fat spread

Wholemeal bread contains lots of fibre, vitamins, and minerals. Also, the energy you get from it lasts longer than energy from white bread. Low-fat dressings and fillings of fresh vegetables and **lean** fresh meats give your body goodness without saturated fat or too many **calories**.

Sweet sandwiches

Sandwiches with sweet fillings, such as jam, honey, or chocolate hazelnut spread, can be tasty for lunch but they are full of sugar, which your body uses up quickly. This can mean your energy level suddenly drops in the afternoon.

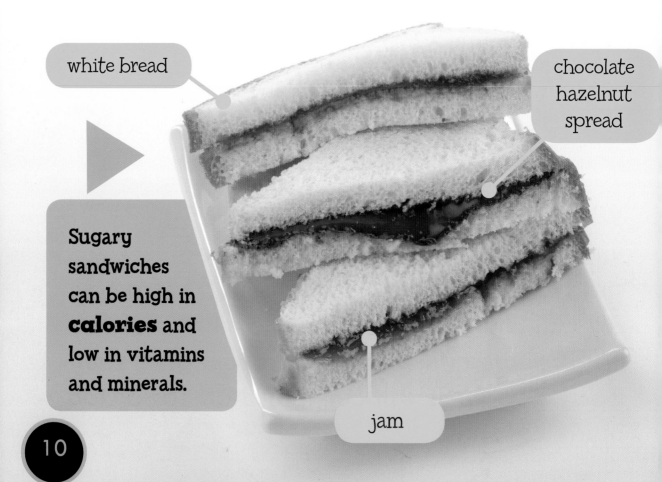

white bread

chocolate hazelnut spread

Sugary sandwiches can be high in **calories** and low in vitamins and minerals.

jam

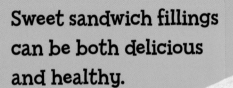

Sweet sandwich fillings can be both delicious and healthy.

wholemeal bread

mashed banana

peanut butter and unsweetened strawberry fruit purée

You can use **wholemeal** bread instead of white bread for energy that lasts longer. There are also sweet fillings you can choose that have both long-lasting energy and lots of **fibre, vitamins,** and **minerals.**

Burgers

If you are in a hurry at lunchtime, you may be tempted to choose a burger and chips from a fast-food restaurant. These are usually high in **saturated fat, sodium,** and **calories.**

Processed foods can contain unhealthy and sometimes harmful **artificial additives**, such as **flavouring, colouring,** and **preservatives.**

fatty chips

white roll

fatty, high-sodium burger

processed cheese

fatty mayonnaise

A burger freshly made from turkey is healthier. Turkey is **leaner** than beef, so it has less saturated fat. It is still rich in **protein**, which your body needs to build skin and muscle. Choose a **wholemeal** roll for **fibre**, with low-fat mayonnaise, and carrot sticks instead of chips, for **vitamins** and **minerals**.

low-fat mayonnaise

turkey burger

lettuce

A grilled burger has much less saturated fat than a fried burger.

tomato

wholemeal roll

Hot dogs

Meat sausages such as hot dogs give our bodies **protein**. However, they are a **processed** food that can be full of **artificial additives** such as **preservatives, colouring,** and **flavouring**. They are also usually high in **saturated fat** and **sodium**.

Hot dogs are a tasty treat, but not healthy as an everyday lunch.

processed sausage

ketchup

white bread

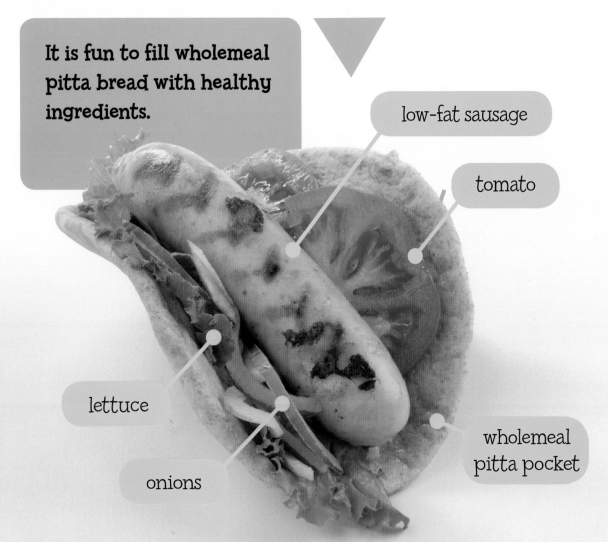

It is fun to fill wholemeal pitta bread with healthy ingredients.

low-fat sausage

tomato

lettuce

onions

wholemeal pitta pocket

Low-fat sausages are a much healthier option. They are still high in protein but much lower in unhealthy saturated fat. Eat them in **wholemeal** pitta bread for longer-lasting energy and lots of **fibre.** Add salad for plenty of **vitamins** and **minerals.**

Chicken

Chicken is a fantastic low-fat source of **protein**. However, coating it and frying it as a nugget makes it high in **saturated fat** and **calories** – especially when eaten with added chips and coleslaw made with full-fat mayonnaise.

Fried chicken may be delicious but it is unhealthy to eat it often.

fried chicken

chips

Make your own healthier nuggets by coating chicken in a mixture of **wholemeal** flour, cornflakes, spices, and a little vegetable oil. Oven-baking them will not add fat. Potato wedges baked with their skin on are also low in fat and high in **fibre**. Make your own coleslaw from low-fat mayonnaise, too.

baked potato wedges with skin on

Ask an adult to help you make your own healthy chicken nugget lunch.

baked chicken nuggets

coleslaw made with low-fat mayonnaise

Noodles and pasta

Just adding boiling water to dried noodles can make a speedy lunch. They give you **carbohydrates** for energy. However, they are a **processed** food which is high in **saturated fat** and **sodium** and low in **vitamins, minerals,** and **fibre**. They also contain unhealthy **artificial additives**.

Instant noodles do not contain much goodness for your body.

artificial **flavouring**

artificial **preservatives**

artificial **colouring**

dried noodles

peas

courgette

red onion

broccoli

wholewheat pasta

potato

tomato

A grown-up can prepare pasta for you almost as quickly as instant noodles.

Wholewheat pasta with fresh vegetables is a healthier choice. Wholewheat pasta gives you long-lasting energy, but it is low in fat and sodium. Fresh vegetables steamed or fried in a little vegetable oil are packed with fibre, vitamins, and minerals. Stir in a little tuna for added **protein.**

Soup

Soup can be a warming lunch on a cold day. However, tinned soup is often high in **sodium** and **artificial additives**. Even some homemade soups, such as creamy fish chowders, can be high in **saturated fat**.

Cheddar and broccoli soup

sour dough bread bowl

Eating your soup with white bread adds **calories** without adding healthy fibre.

A freshly homemade vegetable soup is usually low in fat and sodium but high in **vitamins, minerals,** and healthy **fibre.** If it contains beans, it will be an excellent source of **protein,** too.

Eating your soup with a small **wholemeal** roll will add healthy fibre.

freshly homemade vegetable soup

wholemeal roll

Salads

Salad can be a very healthy choice. However, there are many ingredients that can make salads unhealthy. Shop-bought croutons are high in **saturated fat** and **artificial additives**. Cheese can be high in saturated fat and **sodium**. Creamy dressings such as mayonnaise are high in fat and **calories** too.

croutons

lettuce

Parmesan cheese

creamy Caesar salad dressing

Caesar salad is high in fat and calories.

To keep your salads healthy, include grilled white meat or fish for a low-fat source of **protein**. Use plenty of raw vegetables, fruits, nuts, and seeds, for **fibre**, **vitamins**, **minerals**, and energy. Leave out fatty **red meats**, croutons, cheese, and creamy or very oily dressings.

You can make a healthy salad dressing by mixing balsamic vinegar and olive oil.

raw whole walnuts

lettuce

grapes

grilled chicken

Drinks

Many people like fizzy drinks with their lunch. A can of drink may contain around ten teaspoons of sugar, making it very high in **calories**. Fizzy drinks are also packed with unhealthy additives such as **caffeine**. Diet drinks are just as unhealthy, as they contain lots of **artificial sweetener**, which can be harmful in large quantities.

Drinking lots of fizzy drinks can give you **tooth decay**.

orangeade

lemonade

cola

A small glass of freshly squeezed fruit juice can be a refreshing drink with your lunch. It is packed with **vitamins** and **minerals**. Avoid ready-made fruit juices. They are often full of sugar and **artificial additives**. Water is the healthiest drink of all.

Every bit of your body needs water in order to work properly.

freshly squeezed orange juice

water with fresh orange slices

Food quiz

Take a look at these packed lunches. Can you work out which picture shows an unhealthy lunch and which shows a healthier lunch, and why?

white bread cheese sandwich

chocolate bar

ready-salted crisps

shop-bought fruit juice

The answer is on the next page.

water

wholemeal-bread sandwich with grilled chicken, lettuce, and tomato

carrot sticks and hummus

Food quiz answers

This is the unhealthy lunch. The sandwich is high in **saturated fat, sodium,** and **calories.** The crisps are also high in saturated fat and sodium, and low in **vitamins** and **minerals.** The chocolate bar and the concentrated fruit juice are both high in sugar.

This is the healthy lunch. The **wholemeal** bread sandwich is full of long-lasting energy and **fibre.** The carrot sticks and hummus have plenty of vitamins, minerals, and **protein.** The water will help every bit of your body work properly. Did you guess correctly?

Tips for healthy eating

Use this eatwell plate guide to choose the right amounts of different foods for good health. Choose low-fat cooking methods and do not add salt (it is high in **sodium**). Don't forget to drink several glasses of water and to exercise every day.

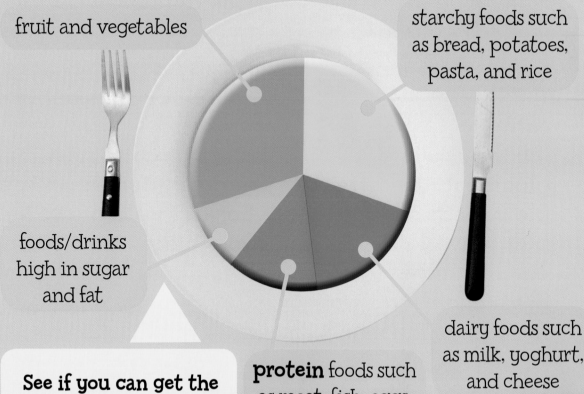

fruit and vegetables

starchy foods such as bread, potatoes, pasta, and rice

foods/drinks high in sugar and fat

dairy foods such as milk, yoghurt, and cheese

See if you can get the right balance over the course of a whole day.

protein foods such as meat, fish, eggs, and beans

Glossary

artificial additive man-made substance that is added to food, such as colouring, flavouring, and preservatives

artificial sweetener man-made substance that can be added to food to give it a sweet taste

caffeine a substance found in parts of some plants, such as coffee plant seeds and tea bush leaves. When eaten, it makes your brain and nerves work faster than is normal.

calorie unit we use for measuring energy

carbohydrate substance in starchy foods (such as potatoes, pasta, and rice) and sugary foods that gives you energy

colouring something added to food to make it look attractive

fibre part of certain plants that passes through your body without being broken down. This helps other foods to pass through your stomach, too. Some fibre can also help your blood stay healthy.

flavouring something added to food to make it taste nicer

lean describes meat which has had the fatty bits trimmed off

mineral natural substance, such as iron, that is essential for health

overweight heavier than is healthy for your age and height

preservative something added to food to make it last longer

processed made or prepared in a factory. Processed foods often contain artificial additives.

protein natural substance that your body needs to build skin, muscle, and other tissues. Protein is found in foods such as meat, fish, and beans.

red meat meat such as beef, lamb, and pork, which is red when raw

saturated fat type of fat found in butter, fatty cuts of meat, cheese, and cream. It is bad for your heart and blood.

sodium a natural substance found in salt

tooth decay bad teeth, caused by the outer layers of the teeth being dissolved away

vitamin natural substance that is essential for good health

wholemeal made with flour that uses every part of the grain, without removing any of the inner or outer bits

wholewheat made with wheat flour that uses every part of the grain, without removing any of the inner or outer bits

Find out more

Books

All About Dairy (Food Zone), Vic Parker (QED, 2010)
A Balanced Diet (Acorn Plus: Healthy Eating), Catherine
  Veitch (Raintree, 2012)
*The Good Green Lunchbox: Tasty, Healthy Lunches and
  Picnics*, Jocelyn Miller (Lion Hudson, 2010)

Websites

Try some healthy recipes at: **www.bbcgoodfood.com/content/
recipes/healthy/healthy-kids**

Try some healthy eating activities at:
www.familylearning.org.uk/balanced_diet.html and **www.bbc.
co.uk/northernireland/schools/4_11/uptoyou/index.shtml**

Find out more about the eatwell plate healthy eating guidelines
at: **www.nhs.uk/Livewell/Goodfood/Pages/eatwell-plate.aspx**

Index